Hand
Shadows

De...
K...

Words by
Sam Smith

Instructions

Find a dark room, then shine a light at the wall and hold your hands in front of it. Look at the pictures closely to see how to place your hands, and move your fingers to bring your shadows to life.

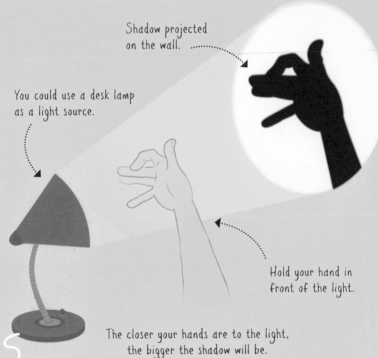

Shadow projected on the wall.

You could use a desk lamp as a light source.

Hold your hand in front of the light.

The closer your hands are to the light, the bigger the shadow will be.

Warm-up exercises

Use these exercises to make your hands more flexible,
and notice the names used for each finger in this book.

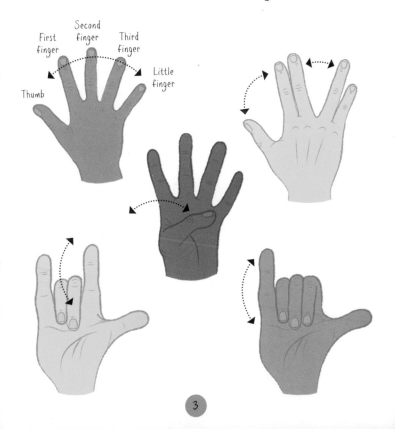

First
finger

Second
finger

Third
finger

Little
finger

Thumb

Curious llama

Twist your wrist to make your llama look around, and lower one pointed finger at a time to turn its ears to listen.

Point your first finger and little finger for the ears.

Excited dog

Make barking noises as you lower and raise your little finger, and move your thumb to twitch its ear.

Curve your first finger for the eye.

Spooky spider

Slowly flex your fingers to wiggle the spider's legs,
and straighten your thumbs to close its huge fangs.

Interlock your
thumbs for
the fangs.

Talking parrot

Try squawking parrot phrases like "Pretty Polly!"
or "Pieces of eight!" in your best parrot voice.

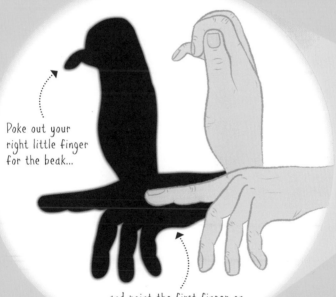

Poke out your
right little finger
for the beak...

... and point the first finger on
your left hand for the perch.

Hooting owl

Don't forget to make hooting noises, and gently move your thumbs to twitch the owl's ear tufts.

The tips of your little fingers drop down to make the eyes.

Slithering snail

Make your snail slowly slither forward, and wiggle your right-hand fingers to wave its eyestalks.

Make a fist for the snail's shell.

Billy goat

Wiggle the bottom fingers of your left hand to show your goat chewing, and do your best billy-goat bleat.

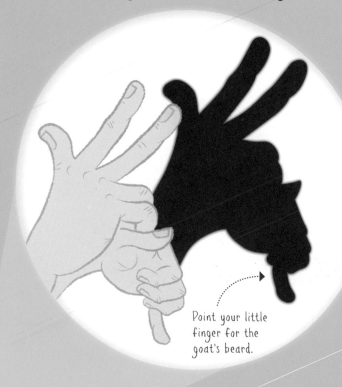

Point your little finger for the goat's beard.

Greedy pig

Make plenty of grunting, oinking and snuffling
noises so your pig sounds nice and greedy.

Leave two fingers
free for the pig's
front legs.

Swimming swan

Straighten your left arm to dip the swan's head for a drink, and flutter your fingers to flick its tail feathers.

Separate your fingers to make the tail feathers.

Bird in flight

Half close and then open your hands to flap the wings, and try out some bird noises, or whistle to make it sing.

Use one thumb for the head and tuck the other one in.

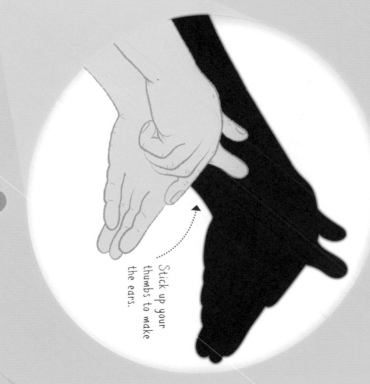

Frisky horse

Move your hands in a quick circle motion to toss the horse's head, and don't forget to neigh!

Stick up your thumbs to make the ears.

Peaceful unicorn

Slowly dip your hands to bow your unicorn's head, and make soft snuffling noises as it noses at the ground.

Point the first finger of your right hand for the horn.

Grunting rhino

Move your thumbs to twitch the rhino's ears, and make some soft snorting and grunting sounds.

Bend your right-hand fingers up for the horn.

Mooing bull

Lower your little finger to open the bull's mouth, then let out a long, low moo.

Point your thumbs up for the bull's horns.

Snapping alligator

Open your hands slowly to reveal a mouth full of huge teeth, then suddenly snap them shut.

Bend some of your fingers for teeth.

Trekking camel

Close your camel's mouth, make its eye a small slit, and make whistling noises as though there's a fierce sandstorm.

Keep your right hand closer to the light so the hump is bigger.

Jumping kangaroo

Tilt your hands forward slightly, and move them up and down to make your kangaroo bounce its way across the wall.

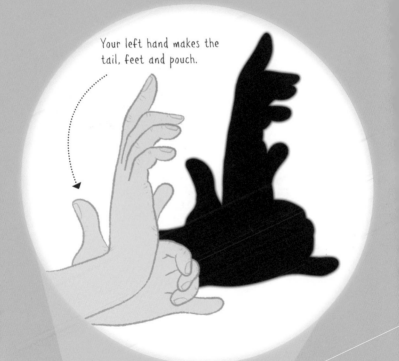

Your left hand makes the tail, feet and pouch.

Relaxed rabbit

Make the rabbit scratch its nose with your right first finger, then wiggle its long ears too.

Use your right hand for the front paws and back legs.

leisurely tortoise

Move the tortoise's legs so that it slowly creeps forward, and raise its head to look around.

Drop two right-hand fingers down for the back legs.

Hungry woodpecker

Jab the air with the woodpecker's beak to show it pecking at insects, and flick its tail feathers too.

Your left hand makes a perch and the tail.

Contented cat

Bend and straighten your first finger to swish your cat's tail, and make some soft purrs and meows.

Slightly raise two knuckles to make the cat's ears.

Barking bulldog

Open the bulldog's mouth as you tilt back its head,
and make it bark loudly at the cat it's just seen.

Your left fist
forms the muzzle.

Snacking squirrel

Raise the squirrel's front paws to its mouth, and make little nibbling noises as it munches on a tasty acorn.

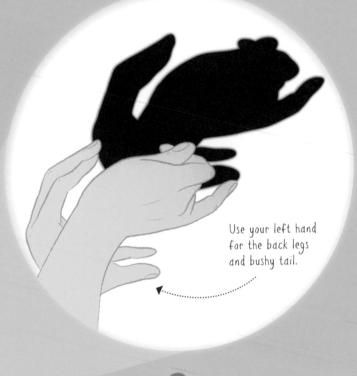

Use your left hand for the back legs and bushy tail.

Bellowing moose

Throw your hands up and backward a little, without changing their position, so the moose tosses its head.

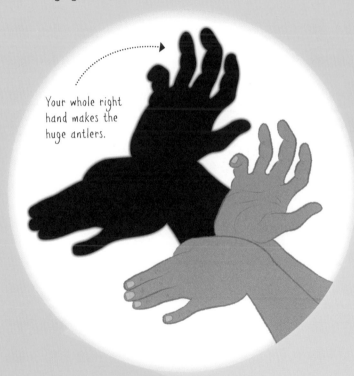

Your whole right hand makes the huge antlers.

Exploring elephant

Flick the elephant's trunk back and forth as it searches for food, then bend your fingers to bring it up to its mouth.

Use your right thumb to make the mouth.

Howling wolf

Tilt back your wolf's head, open its mouth a little, and let out a long, hair-raising howl.

Tuck your first fingers in above the muzzle.

Quacking duck

Open and close the duck's beak and make lots
of loud honking and quacking noises.

Tuck your third finger
in under your thumb.

Grazing deer

Dip your hands to lower the deer's head, and move your
bottom two fingers to show it chewing on some grass.

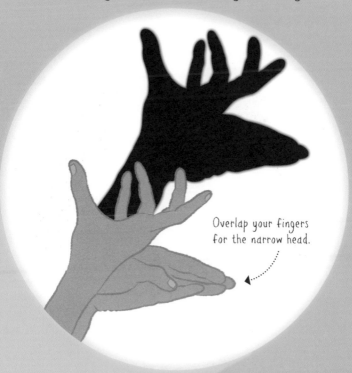

Overlap your fingers
for the narrow head.

Shadow stories

You could try making two shadows at once,
or a series of different ones to tell a story.